THIS BOOK IS DEDICATED TO

THOSE WHO ARE PRIVILEGED TO BE CHOSEN

TO LEAD

COMMUNITY NONPROFIT ORGANIZATIONS

OR

FOR-PROFIT BUSINESSESS

THAT THEY CAN BE THE GIFT OF CHANGE

THAT BRINGS HOPE

TO OUR WORLD

ACKNOWLEDGEMENT

A special debt of gratitude to my beautiful wife, Katherine, without whose support this book could not be written; and my sister-in-law, Amy, who brought love and hope to this effort.

My sincere thanks to our three sons, Troy, Brad, and Ethan; and to our niece, Ursula Quan, and our nephew, Michael Cooper, who followed their hopes and turned their journeys into rare blessings of wisdom that now provide the insights critical to this book.

Admiration to Irv Cockett, Al Pauole and Michael Beasley for their keen wisdom and genuine support through jubilant and difficult times, but principally for their friendship.

Many thanks to my wife, Katherine, who designed the front and back covers with impeccable skill.

Appreciation to all the volunteers, especially Herb Lee, who served the Pacific American Foundation with great passion and competence; their commitment and skills have ensured for many a quality of life that would have not been possible otherwise.

A great deal of esteem and respect to the superb staff of The Hana Group, Inc., at Honolulu, HI; Wayne, PA; and Alexandria, VA - Troy Cooper; Brad Cooper; Ethan Cooper; Tom Murphy; Ursula Quan; Joyce Randazzo; Steve Carmine; Mike Beasley; Michael Cooper; Cliff Metaxa; Kenneth Fisher; Michael Rawlins; Andrew Dash; Herb Bactad; Amanda Cooper; Diana Stephens; Jared Smith; Pablo Crespo; Dominic Magee, Vladimir Cadet - whose loyalty, knowledge, and passion have been substantially responsible for the successes of Hui O Hana Pono.

A special Aloha to family and friends who have been supportive these many years – Bonnie, Kawai, Kaimi, Kanoa, Kimi, Debbie, Pat Contrades, Lisa Curtin and Colby Curtin.

A heartfelt mahalo to all my mentors and colleagues: Zelma Baker; Ralph Haines; William Rosson; Carl Stiner; Don Rosenblum; Larry Zimmerman; Jim Ranallo; Stephen Dakoff; Kenneth F. Brown; Robert Oshiro; Dan Inouye; Jim and Helen Hall; Mike and Molly Akin; Maggie Gervais; Lynn Wong; Andrew Poepoe; Michael Youth; Dean Hoe; Ann Murata - who over the many years unselfishly shared their wisdom, time, patience and most of all their friendship.

Finally, apologies to anyone not mentioned in this Acknowledgement.

FOREWORD

After more than 24 years of capturing the many factors – values, economics, financial, social, marketing, branding, reputation, leadership, management, governance - that impact both a community nonprofit organization and a for-profit business concern, the picture of what it takes to be successful at each began to take shape.

There were more common traits shared by both community nonprofit organizations and for-profit business concerns than there were dissimilarities.

Traditionally, foundations were formed as independent organizations with a social mission and dependent on contributions from like-minded people or other private charities, while leveraging the funding programs by national governments and State or local legislatures.

Additionally, investing a foundation's resources to secure a greater return is an honored method to build wealth that allowed the foundation to continue its social mission.

Nearly all major corporations and international conglomerates include a nonprofit mission in their governance structure; the tax advantages and charitable intentions of a corporation are included as a benefit gained in advancing and enhancing the corporate's principal product or service; oftentimes the corporate nonprofit division's mission statement is closely affiliated to the corporation's principal business concern - wealth creation and wealth maintenance.

The distinction between the corporation and its internal nonprofit division is purposely blurred by the connection of their purposes; there is no arms-length decision making process as the corporate leadership appoints the Executive Director of their corporate nonprofit division. It is a corporate social responsibility that is quite different from a community social accountability.

The disconnects between (1) corporate wealth building and wealth maintenance, its corporate nonprofit divisions and investment portfolios; and (2) community nonprofits designed and managed to address a human condition present a startling picture of leading and managing each organization to success and what it takes to achieve that success.

There is, however, an uncommon bridge that links for-profit corporations and community nonprofit organizations within a different framework that honors cultural values while dedicating itself to creating wealth, but with an honorable devotion to wealth distribution and selfless service.

Thus, the aim of this book is to capture the bridge of "what works" through a series of business case analyses of the decisions reached by the Board of Directors, Pacific American Foundation, 1993-2004, and the Board of Directors, Hui O Hana Pono, 2004-2017, the Native Hawaiian Organization (NHO), as they campaigned to develop the cultural and economic self-sufficiency of an indigenous group, Native Hawaiians, who live today in many parts of our great country.

The business case analyses reflect a 21st century model far different than many of us realized – a battle for the soul of for-profit companies fortified with the heart of nonprofit values.

The experiences gained from leading and managing both a community nonprofit organization, The Pacific American Foundation, and for-profit businesses, Hui O Hana Pono, characterized as small businesses as well as designated 8(a) companies focused primarily on government business and commercial companies designed for wealth management and real estate, provide a comparison of earned values.

The similarities of success are more common between each other than we believe.

"What works" will also help inform the journey for self-determination for Native Hawaiians by Native Hawaiians, within the framework that what is good for Native Hawaiians is also good for all Americans. Our Nation believes in equal treatment of all its citizens, and the presumption is bound in our Constitution that all Americans, especially Native indigenous peoples, are to be respected for their cultures and values that help our Nation be what it is today, and can be tomorrow.

The Native Hawaiian path started in 1921 with a political action to resuscitate Native Hawaiians whose population, from a high of approximately 300,000 when Captain James Cook anchored at Kealakekua Bay in 1778, fell to a devastatingly low of approximately 40,000 in 1920.

Economics empowers and energizes political will; and together they stimulate, generate and produce the public policy that can create meaningful measures of self-determination by villages, towns and communities, as well as for Native Hawaiians in their quest for self-determination or their battle over the elements of sovereignty.

The focus of this book is to share the leadership and management strengths of the economic engines indigenous to both the community nonprofit organizations and the for-profit businesses, with hopes that the journey for self-determination will be broaden and thus available to many more.

And consequently advance the hope of respect and peace throughout the world.

TABLE OF CONTENTS

Army Tree Trimming

Chapter 1. The Early Years, 1984 – 1993: Strategic Concepts

Council on Foreign Relations (CFR)

This narrative goes back in time, 1984-1985, to the Council on Foreign Relations (CFR), founded on 29 July 1921 in New York City, by Colonel Edward Madell House, Chief Advisor to President Woodrow Wilson, a current 4900-member nonprofit organization, publisher of the bi-monthly Foreign Affairs Journal, think-tank and convening authority specializing in U.S. foreign policy and international affairs presently housed at 58 East 68th Street, New York City, NY.

The Council on Foreign Relations (CFR) in New York City maintains an impeccable reputation for its authority as a convening organization; its erudite quarterly publication, Foreign Affairs Journal; its daily luncheons featuring guest speakers widely recognized for their competence in economics, finance, banking, international and national politics, corporate and government leadership and management; noted authors, researchers and academics; innovative thinkers in social dynamics; and sitting foreign leaders whose world views may often be at odds with American principles of democracy.

The CFR generally hosts daily invitation-only lunches in the paneled Library; sponsors many study groups, one of which led to a publication in 1987, Turkey: America's Forgotten Ally, by Dankwart A. Rustow; featured evening speakers followed by exciting discussions; and brought together superb business, political, social and economic leaders and brilliant researchers in several fields who collaborated on the stimulating research projects supported by the outstanding staff members and Fellows.

Currently, the CFR hosts about six different Fellowships annually, such as the Military Fellowship, International Affairs Fellowships, IAF in Canada, IAF in Japan, IAF in International Economics and the Stanton Nuclear Security Fellowship. These Fellowships are normally competitive and selection of the Fellows is made by a Committee of distinguished, active CFR members along with the CFR staff executives.

Two events gave rise and helped shape the quest to building an instrument, relevant to Native Hawaiians and other indigenous groups, that not only housed and revealed a significant, noteworthy past, but was also capable of properly navigating life's changes while maintaining a true course of providing opportunities that have a positive impact on our villages, towns, communities and country.

The first occurred during a CFR white-glove lunch for the President of American Express who spoke, and took questions, on various intersections of the financial business and national policies with which the leaders of American Express were most interested.

Listening to the vibrant discussion, it dawned on the audience that public policies impacted the financial sustainability of a business, and therefore it had to be also true that financial considerations played a significant part to the approach and in the language of public policy.

Which factor came first or influenced the other really did not matter, as they were intertwined just as national pronouncements were to international policies, or national policies to international pronouncements.

They both mattered.

But it wasn't until January 1994, ten years later, that the second event occurred; and it made the connectivity of sustainable business and public policies suddenly real, alive and material.

Cultural and Business Leaders in Hawaii

The connectivity happened with Kahu Abraham Akaka's (Pastor, Kawaiaha'o Church, Honolulu, Hawaii) comment in the afternoon of January 1994 in Honolulu, Hawaii that he had asked Booze Allen Hamilton from San Francisco, 30 years earlier, to define who Native Hawaiians are, where Native Hawaiians needed to go, and how Native Hawaiians, with appropriate help, can get there.

Kahu Akaka, a Native Hawaiian leading thinker and doer in the State of Hawaii, believed that the culture and future of Native Hawaiians, principally in the State of Hawaii, were adrift and had been objectively rudderless in accommodating the many political, economic, education, and social changes that had come to the shores of Hawaii.

Hence, he took steps to invite reputable consultants to examine the status of and future for Native Hawaiians.

In speaking with his *Tutuwahine* (Grandmother), Kahu Akaka, then a young adult in 1935, asked a seemingly innocent question of his *Tutuwahine*– why were all the Hawaiian Gods dying – to which his *Tutuwahine*, who had never traveled more than 50 miles outside her home, replied:

> The Hawaiian Gods are dying because they never went to New York City.

Amazingly, she intuitively knew that New York City in the 1930's was the hub of creative thinking in foreign policy; innovative ideas in educational, social, governance, military and public policy; center of strategic financial concepts; inspired cultural philosophies; and the not-too-subtle exercise of power. New York City was the center of change because it created changes.

She expressed her belief that many critical changes were coming to Hawaii's shores, and the Native Hawaiian Gods were blind, perhaps uncaring, to recognize, understand and then accommodate the changes.

Native Hawaiians belief in their Gods was nearing despair and perhaps dejection and darkness.

Kahu Akaka gave voice to what many other leaders in Hawaii had apparently been thinking – how to preserve the culture and the indigenous Native Hawaiian people of the Islands of Hawaii.

Princess Bernice Pauahi Bishop; Mary Kawena Pukui; Kenneth F. Brown, Bob Oshiro, Myron Thompson, and David EK Cooper were business as well as cultural leaders whose handprints were visible on a number of efforts to improve the well-being of Native Hawaiians.

Princess Bernice Pauahi Bishop founded the Kamehameha Schools; Mary Kawena Pukui as the preeminent scholar on Native Hawaiian culture and traditions; Kenneth Brown occupied the Chair, Queens Healthcare Systems; Bob Oshiro was the Executive Director, Queen Emma Foundation; Myron Thompson served as a Trustee, Bishop Estate; and David EK Cooper founded and was the first President, Pacific American Foundation.

However, there were many Native Hawaiians and others, who provided direct support, guidance and resources to advance the preservation of Native Hawaiian culture – Kumu Hula, teachers who were everywhere in the world, who taught the ancient and modern dances reflective of Native Hawaiian culture; cultural leaders who replicated the voyages of the original Native Hawaiian settlers of the Islands of Hawaii; linguistic teachers who taught the language of Native Hawaiians in our schools and universities; educational administrators who maintained the cultural foundations of the indigenous Native Hawaiians; composers and artists whose skills captured forever the splendor of Native Hawaiians and the passionate beauty of the Islands; and those who went before, as Samuel Kamakau and David Malo, who recognized that the battle for Native Hawaiian preservation had already begun in their time.

Preservation of the Native Hawaiians and their culture was not a new issue, for in 1920 the United States Congress, at the urging of Prince Jonah Kalaniana'ole Kuhio (1871-1922), Hawaii's Delegate to the United States Congress, passed the Hawaiian Homes Commission Act of 1921 that was signed into law by President Warren G. Harding.

At the time of the Act, there were reportedly less than 40,000 Native Hawaiians, a decline by nearly 260,000, or 75%, of the Native Hawaiian population when in 1778 Captain James Cook sailed into Kealakekua Bay in the Big Island of Hawaii.

The purpose of the Act, setting aside approximately 200,000 acres as a land trust for homesteading by Native Hawaiians, was to rehabilitate Native Hawaiians by returning them to the land in order to maintain their traditional ties to the land and nature, to support self-sufficiency and self-determination, and the preservation of their culture, traditions and values.

Delegate Jonah Kalaniana'ole Kuhio was instrumental in persuading the United States Congress to pass, and President Harding to sign, the Hawaiian Homes Commission Act of 1921.

The plight of Native Hawaiians was not resolved by the Act, for it contained high blood quantum requirements and leased land rather than granting it outright as fee simple.

This act, and others like it, continue to be controversial in modern Hawaii politics; and it created a movement to recognize self-determination by Native Hawaiians and the appropriate principles of sovereignty for Native Hawaiians.

In 1993, seventy-two (72) years after the Hawaiian Homes Commission Act of 1921, United States Public Law 103-150, informally known as the Apology Resolution, was passed as a Joint Resolution by both the United States Senate and the United States House of Representatives and signed by President Bill Clinton on November 23, 1993.

It acknowledges that the:

> Overthrow of the Kingdom of Hawaii occurred with the active participation of agents and citizens of the United States and further acknowledges that the Native Hawaiian people never directly relinquished to the United States their claims to their inherent sovereignty as a people over their national lands, either through the Kingdom of Hawaii or through a plebiscite or referendum.

The Apology Resolution had been subject to various explanations, oftentimes serious and intense debate, and had taken its place as a major impetus for the

Native Hawaiian movement of recognition for self-determination by Native Hawaiians and the appropriate principles of sovereignty for Native Hawaiians.

Seventy-five (75) years later, in 1996 an article entitled "The Quest for Sovereignty in the Pacific," published by The Pacific Institute/The Asia Institute, was part of a series of essays in the book, <u>Taiwan Independence and Limitations to the Nation-State Concept</u>, and presented in Japan as part of a series of discussions on sovereignty, Kenneth F. Brown commented in the Foreword to the article that:

> It was not so long ago that the very idea of self-determination for Native Hawaiians by Native Hawaiian was synonymous with futility and shrugged off as pure fantasy by so many. In the swift surge of a powerful wave that had been building for more than one hundred and three years and is poised to crest, the Native Hawaiian sovereignty movement has become a matter of national interest.

The author of the essay described the Native Hawaiian quest for self-determination by Native Hawaiians, and the appropriate principles of sovereignty for Native Hawaiians, rather decisively:

> Economic restitution may well be the biggest single hurdle in the process; yet it is the most insignificant and least important if its debate is to provide immediate, personal compensation to individual Native Hawaiians....

> Land is the engine of sovereignty...the return of thousands of acres ... would provide the economic stability and momentum for their solutions to improved health care, improved education, improved leadership skills, improved

participation in the process of government at all levels, improved standard of living, and the sustainment of their culture. The income that can be derived from lease agreements with federal and state agencies and commercial corporations, from planned development projects, and from investment strategies is simply staggering.

Economic power – who should have it and how it is to be used – is the real war being waged today by various groups on behalf of Native Hawaiian sovereignty. Claimants today must understand the moral responsibility such power demands, for without a passionate commitment to integrity, wisdom and service the quest for Native Hawaiian sovereignty will never pass the most important test of all – the American people.

Already there were credible arguments surfacing in the background that political will alone cannot be the end all.

Political will must be interwoven with an economic engine, and both had to be fixed to a valid, binding process to legitimize the path to self-determination.

As the author declared,

> ...the will of the Native Hawaiian people must wind its way through acceptances by the legally constituted governments of the State of Hawai'i and the United States of America.
>
> The path to legitimize sovereignty for Native Hawaiians, as Native Americans, passes through the people of Hawaii, the people of America, and the United States Congress.

The author concludes the article with a summation:

> Juxtapose the principles and the process of sovereignty successfully applied to Native American Indians as described earlier with the historical elements outlined above for Native Hawaiians and the conclusion ought to be that all indigenous peoples share the same inherent rights of sovereignty. Within the political responsibilities and geographical boundaries of the United States, there are no other legitimate indigenous peoples than the American Indians, Alaskan Natives and Native Hawaiians.

The next major quest for preservation of the values, traditions and culture of Native Hawaiians came in the United States Senate and House of Representative's battle to pass the Native Hawaiian Reorganization Act of 2009 (S1011/HR2314), a time difference of eighty-eight years after the Hawaiian Homes Commission Act of 1921.

The Native Hawaiian Reorganization Act of 2009 is commonly referred to as the Akaka Bill.

The stated purpose of the Akaka Bill is:

> ... to provide a process for the reorganization of the single Native Hawaiian governing entity and the reaffirmation of the special political and legal relationship between the United States and the Native Hawaiian entity for the purposes of continuing a government-to-government relationship.

First introduced in 2000, the Akaka Bill had endured several setbacks and false starts far too numerous to outline in this book, but a good summary can be found in many references, as Wikipedia, for example.

After years of Congressional maneuvering, the Akaka Bill died in 2009 on the floor of the United States Congress.

In December 2010 Senator Daniel K. Akaka, a graduate of The Kamehameha Schools and the brother of Kahu Abraham Akaka, took the floor of the U.S. Senate and declared that the failure of the Akaka Bill lay at the feet of "misleading attacks" and "unprecedented obstruction."

Today, 2017, ninety-six (96) years since the passage of the Hawaiian Homes Commission Act of 1921, the future outlook for positive political legislative action has dimmed considerably.

It was not a far reach, then, to have started this journey in November 1993 with the nonprofit organization, The Pacific American Foundation (PAF).

It was the beginning of a journey that had no financial objectives nor an end-date; its basic philosophy was to bring hope to all Americans who could trace their ancestry to the indigenous Pacific peoples, that they could stand with one foot solidly in their cultures and the other foot solidly planted as citizens of the United States of America.

In 2004, the intersection of providing hope occurred with the announcement that the U.S. Small Business Administration had approved the status of the Native Hawaiian Organization (NHO) with nearly the same Federal Acquisition Regulations (FAR) contractual privileges as the Native American Tribes and the Alaskan Native Corporations.

The NHO was to be formed as a registered, State of Hawaii-approved nonprofit organization with for-profit companies aligned to it as its economic engine.

What was a small seed that had taken root in 1984 at the Council on Foreign Relations (CFR) in New York City now had blossomed in 2004 into an authorized business structure for the indigenous Native Hawaiians, business firms that were strategically managed by a State-approved nonprofit organization, a structure similar to a hospital healthcare system which has a nonprofit governing structure with for-profit subsidiaries.

It is interesting to note that in approximately 1935, Kahu Akaka's Tutuwahine cited New York City as the reason why the Native Hawaiian Gods were dying; and in 1984, 49 years later, at a luncheon at the Council on Foreign Relations in New York City, hope was again resuscitated.

Thus was born the for-profit companies owned and governed by a nonprofit organization, the perfect alignment to shape the journey of hope, the quest for self-determination by villages, towns, communities and Native Hawaiians with appropriate principles of sovereignty for Native Hawaiians, one of the United States three (3) indigenous groups...Indian Tribes, Alaskan Natives, and Native Hawaiians.

Business Case Methodology

Through the business case methodology approach, the similarities of leading and managing a community nonprofit organization and a for-profit firm, in terms of values and wealth creation, should be readily perceptible, just as the dissimilarities should be somewhat easily recognizable.

There are, however, more alikeness and resemblances than wrongness and differences.

The analyses will focus on the Pacific American Foundation, as the community nonprofit organization, and the Native Hawaiian Organization, Hui O Hana Pono, as the for-profit business.

More specifically, the decision making process of both Boards of each organization as they wrestled with all the nuances of leadership values, management techniques, business processes, Federal and State regulations, budgets, accounting, external and internal financial audits, Federal and State Tax returns, financial strategies, grant writing, Request for Proposal (RFP) technical and pricing proposals, surveys, investigations, inquiries, reviews and analyses, market research, risk management, insurances, security classification levels, unions and Collective Bargaining Agreements, union grievances, technological innovations, business development, recruiting volunteers and skilled employees, time sheet and payroll software programs, environmental concerns, legal issues, law suits, training in classrooms and online, travel policy and travel voucher accounting rules, web sites, social media, and all forms of communication, among many others.

Fortunately for the business case analyses, the members of the PAF Board of Directors and the Hui O Hana Pono Board of Directors over the past twenty-two (22) years have been principally the same Native Hawaiians, David EK Cooper, Irwin K. Cockett, and Alvin H. Pauole, who formed the core of the decision making process.

Hence, the value factors and business factors that form the matrix of the analysis will have the consistency, constancy, uniformity and reliability so important to the validity of the findings and conclusions.

The business case analyses will focus on six factors below:

1. Governance
2. Financial Strategy
3. Accounting and External Audit
4. Human Resources
5. Operations
6. Conclusions

Chapter 2. The Nonprofit Years, 1993 – 2004

The Pacific American Foundation (PAF)

In November 1993 the application papers for the Pacific American Foundation (PAF) as a 501(c)(3) were submitted to the Internal Revenue Service; and in March 1994 the application was approved by the IRS which made the Pacific American Foundation a legally valid nonprofit organization with the purpose to improve the lives of Pacific Americans – American Samoans, Fijians, Chamorros, Maoris, Native Hawaiians, Tahitians and Tongans – Americans who were proud to be Americans and also proud of their Pacific ancestral cultures.

Being a legally valid 501(c)(3) was just the first step of a nonprofit organization with a purpose of selfless service to seven (7) ethnicities of Pacific Americans with somewhat different cultures, though similar in their philosophies of governance, importance of family, music, and traditions.

In March 1994 there was little thought given to funding, branding, governance, grant writing, support of communities, past performances, volunteers, staff experience, accounting, and annual 990 audits - all elements that were required to being effectively and efficiently competitive in the nonprofit world.

Currently in its twenty-third (23) year of operation, the PAF has been a significant influence in serving all its constituents.

And as a recognition of PAF's outstanding work, in 2013 the White House invited the serving Executive Director to receive the "Cesar Chavez Champion of Change" award along with nine other outstanding nonprofit organizations in the nation.

Today, PAF is being led by a phenomenal leader and a superb Board of Directors; together they have continued the outstanding work done by the many earlier and current volunteers who worked long arduous hours on numerous activities and asked for nothing in return; they are the true heroes who selflessly gave of their time and skills on projects across the range of needs of their constituents:

1. Conducting the first ever Pacific American Healthcare Summit in the Summer of 1994 in Honolulu attended by American Samoan, Chamorro and Native Hawaiian healthcare, political, business and community leaders which led to the seminal report, "Pacific Americans and the National Health Care Act: Where We Fit," that was hand delivered to each of the 535 members of the United States Congress in the Fall of 1994.

2. Developing the cultural leadership program that is now the National Pacific American Leadership Institute (NAPALI) and in its twentieth consecutive year of hosting a cultural leadership course for Pacific American emerging leaders from across the country.

3. Designing a Hawaii Department of Education-approved curriculum based on Native Hawaiian scholarship focused on STEM disciplines using the fishponds *(loko ia)* as the teaching vehicle.

4. Rebuilding ancient fishponds, as *Kahinapohaku Loko Ia*, consistent with Native Hawaiian engineering skills, on the island of Moloka'i with the Federal funding support from the EPA and direct involvement of Moloka'i Native Hawaiians leadership and fishpond workforce.

5. Re-planting and re-nourishing Native Hawaiian indigenous plants, in cooperation with the Fish and Wildlife Agency, to protect the sand dunes of Moloka'i.

6. Studying minority health centers in Washington and Oregon to pinpoint their governance and operational best practices in a report shared with the five Native Hawaiian healthcare community centers funded through Papa Ola Lokahi by the Department of Health and Human Services' Minority Healthcare Office.

7. Establishing mentoring programs for Pacific American high school students on Kaua'i and the Big Island of Hawaii.

8. Increasing decision-making by Pacific American high school students through use of the Kuder Program that aligns the strengths of the student with the career assessments in the technology, corporate and industry fields; the focus was to increase the attendance of Pacific American students at universities and colleges across the nation.

9. Leading the honoring of our Pacific Veterans at the annual "Roll Call of Honor," now in its nineteenth (19) consecutive year, a celebration held on the last Sunday of May beginning at 0900 at the Native American tree planted by the current CEO of Hui O Hana Pono, Arlington National Cemetery, nineteen years ago; and followed six (6) hours later by a celebration at 0900 at the National Pacific Memorial Cemetery at Honolulu, HI.

10. Establishing an Internship Program during the summer with Harvard University for two (2)

Master Degree students who were beginning their course studies in Business Administration or Social Work.

11. Opening a brick and mortar retail, website and an online ordering cultural art center that featured works from Pacific American artists, as, bowls and trays made from monkey pod and other types of wood, oil and acrylic painting, photographic cards and even a homemade tin canoe.

12. Leading a study for the American Fijians in Sacramento, CA in their quest for valid immigration status.

The list of achievements above is but a highlight of the many, many positive initiatives PAF undertook in accomplishing its purpose; the resulting benefits continue to this very day.

The Pacific American Foundation built bridges of cooperation and collaboration with various communities, educational, corporate and nonprofit entities; and in this process gained valuable insights to the requirements and needs of Pacific Americans, especially Native Hawaiians.

The ability to reach out and communicate effectively at all levels by PAF's leadership was an authentic, esteemed and prized strength much appreciated by the communities PAF served.

Business Case Analyses of Four PAF Projects

1. Pacific Americans and the National Healthcare Act: Where We Fit

In the spring of 1994, the Founder and then-President of PAF met with the Board of Directors, Queens Healthcare Systems in their conference room on the 23rd floor of the building on the corner of Alakea and Merchant Streets, Honolulu, HI.

It was the very first PAF business development session focused on a single purpose – to request funding support from the Queens Healthcare Systems Board to host a Pacific American Healthcare Summit for American Samoan, Chamorro and Native Hawaiian healthcare, political, business and community leaders in Hawaii which would lead to the seminal report, "Pacific Americans and the National Health Care Act: Where We Fit," that would then be hand delivered to each of the 535 members of the United States Congress in the Fall of 1994.

In attendance at the seminal session were Kenneth F. Brown, Chair, Queens Healthcare Systems; Bob Oshiro, Executive Director, Queen Emma Foundation; Ivan Lui-Kwan and Bob Ozaki, Directors, Queens Healthcare Systems.

Governance. The immediate questions involved the authenticity of the Pacific American Foundation which led to the presentation of the original IRS-approval letter and the registration of the PAF as a nonprofit organization in the State of Virginia, as Virginia had the most favorable regulations concerning the Officers and Directors of a nonprofit organization.

The concern of the Board seemed to focus on ensuring that the PAF Officers and Directors were reputable people with leadership skills and a value of commitment.

It was clearly important to the Queens Healthcare

Systems Board that the PAF Officers and Directors were principally not only residents of Hawaii but also Native Hawaiians; the PAF Officers and Board members, at least two of us, passed with flying colors. This factor, however, was not even a concern in preparing for the presentation of the project to the Queens Healthcare Systems Board; it was not on the radar screen.

But undoubtedly it was a significant factor to the Queens Healthcare Systems Board, for if they approved the request for funding, they wanted to be sure that their funding was not going into a black hole; they were hesitant to put their personal reputation, and that of the Queens Healthcare Systems, on the line unless they knew the reputation of the PAF Officers and Directors.

A telling question asked by Bob Oshiro was a clear signal that the primary concern of the Queens Healthcare Systems Board was, "Who is the Pacific American Foundation?"

In looking back at that session of twenty-four years ago, it was not the weeks of preparation nor the presentation itself nor the actions leading to the conference nor the end report delivered to 535 members of the United States Congress.

It was simply the reputation of the PAF Officers and Directors that was validated by the Board members of Queens Healthcare Systems, a reputation developed through historical trust and confidence built over long political and social relationships.

The result ended in the Queens Healthcare Systems Board's immediate approval of a six-figure contribution for the PAF to host its Pacific American Healthcare Summit in the summer of 1994.

Financial Strategy. Determining a funding amount was not considered as an important factor of the presentation; thus when the question was asked how much did the PAF need to conduct the Summit and prepare the report, the answer was purely a guess; there was no thought given to identifying a budget for each major event – Summit, travel cost for those coming from American Samoa and Guam; office space; administrative assistance; preparation and printing of the report; there was also no consideration given to the estimated cost of accounting, salaries, taxes, accounting, banking accounts and external audit.

But, the Summit also was an appropriate fit for the mission of Queens Healthcare Systems and was seen by all those in attendance as a very suitable, proper and right project to support financially and lend their reputation to the effort.

Therefore, the contribution amount approved by the Board of Queens Healthcare Systems was more than generous and sufficient.

The planning and execution support provided by various staff members of Queens Healthcare Systems and Queen Emma Foundation, and the suite of offices provided by the law firm, Carlsmith Ball, and the dedication by Chamorro, Native Hawaiian and American Samoan leaders made the first ever PAF project magical.

Accounting and External Audit. Because this project proposal and request for funding was frankly an impromptu decision, PAF had no infrastructure in place; there was little advance thought given as to (1) how to account for the contribution (2) the accounting and verification of invoices (3) payments by checks (4) salaries (5) State and Federal taxes (6) Workers

Compensation insurance, (7) audit procedures, and (8) an indirect cost rate approved by a principal Federal agency.

There was not even a bank account with a signature card in place at either Bank of Hawaii, First Hawaiian Bank, or American Security Bank.

Human Resources. There was no Human Resources department nor a Director; PAF had no event planners, nor facilitators and certainly no project manager; there was neither a payroll program nor an office program for recording vacation time earned and taken nor was there a Change of Status form or offer letter with the proper job description and exempt or non-exempt status; there were certainly challenges to execute PAF's first activity.

Operations. The PAF had not thought of volunteers; it was an organization that was emerging.

Conclusions. There are four factors learned from this very first PAF project:

1. In its first request for funding support to kick off its first ever project, PAF did not have many factors necessary for a successful outcome, except a positive attitude.

2. PAF had no relevant past performance, embraced an appreciation for a financial strategy, understood it needed an accounting and human resources programs, and realized the many challenges it faced to execute operationally the project.

3. But PAF, an emerging nonprofit organization, did have a governance structure that was meaningful to the Queens Healthcare Systems

Board. But it did rely on past relationships and understood the importance of relationships built on confidence and trust.

4. And it did select a project with a national urgency that reverberated to a group of leaders, who were not only concerned about improving health care for an underserved population, but also focused on improving the quality of their lives; the Pacific American Foundation found the right audience.

2.   <u>Minority Healthcare Centers – Best Practices and Techniques</u>

In 1995-1996, the Pacific American Foundation continued its focus on minority healthcare, but it was more seasoned and experienced based on its first project which was successfully concluded with the hand delivery of the report, "Pacific Americans and the National Healthcare Act: Where We Fit," to every one of the 535 members of the United States Congress in the fall of 1994.

The end state of the second healthcare project was a report based on the best practices and techniques of healthcare centers that focused principally on their underserved minority populations.

The purpose of the report was to inform the five Native Hawaiian healthcare centers, one each on the islands of Oahu, Moloka'i, Hawaii, Kaua'i and Maui, and managed by Papa Ola Lokahi, how best to be more effective and efficient in their management, financial accountability, operations and community outreach.

Governance. Alvin H. Pauole, a Native Hawaiian from Hanalei, Kaua'i, and a graduate of the Kamehameha School for Boys, Class of 1956, and the United States

Naval Academy, Class of 1960, had joined the Pacific American Foundation in 1995 as its Executive Director.

Also joining PAF as its principal Native Hawaiian cultural advisor was Likeke Paglinawan, former Executive Director, Office of Hawaiian Affairs (OHA).

Additionally, the following three Native Hawaiians joined the Pacific American Foundation Board of Directors: Clint Helenihi, a graduate of the Kamehameha School for Boys, Class of 1955, and a retired Naval Master Chief; Kenneth F. Brown, Chairman, Queens Healthcare Systems, who traced his ancestry to Papa I'i, the chief advisor to King Kamehameha; and Ivan Lui-Kwan, principal attorney, Carlsmith Ball, and also a Director, Queens Healthcare Systems.

Robert Oshiro, Executive Director, Queen Emma Foundation, at the request of the President, PAF, provided an office space at no cost to PAF in the Queen Emma Foundation suite of offices on Piikoi Street, Honolulu, Hawaii. The President, PAF, and Likeke Paglinawan worked out of this office for nearly two years.

Mike Beasley remained as the Secretary and General Counsel of the PAF Board, positions he has continuously held since the beginning of the Foundation.

Financial Strategy. The Pacific American Foundation began to think through a 10-year financial strategy, realizing that the contribution to fund the 1994 Pacific American Healthcare Summit and the follow-on report, "Pacific Americans and the National Health Care Act: Where We Fit," was a sample of how PAF could raise revenue to accomplish its purposes.

PAF began its collaboration with the Hawaii Delegation to Congress, and it was the late Senator Daniel Inouye and Representative Patsy Mink, United States Congress, who suggested a link to the Federal grant system that provided funds to support community nonprofit projects focused on minority education, healthcare and environmental initiatives.

While PAF's leadership consulted with its Board regarding other Hawaii community nonprofit organizations that served principally Native Hawaiians and how PAF could complement their work, PAF's leadership believed a continuation of its first initiative in healthcare would be productive.

Hence, the President of PAF, working with the Queen Emma Foundation, submitted a grant for its second project, "Minority Healthcare Centers – Best Practices and Techniques."

Queen Emma Foundation Board approved PAF's request to fund its second project, and the work began in 1995.

Accounting and External Audit. Michael Beasley, General Counsel to PAF, recommended an accountant to prepare, maintain and account for PAF's inflows and outflows.

The independent accountant was hired, and not only maintained the accounting in accordance with GAAP, but also prepared the Federal 990 tax return, developed a payroll program that was in compliance with regulations as well as coordinated with a Maryland auditing firm that audited PAF's accounting system from 1996-2004.

The President, PAF, worked closely with the accountant on every revenue generated, invoiced and paid as well as the preparation and conduct of the external audit and follow-on audit report. Finances and accounting were a principal responsibility of the President, PAF.

Human Resources. PAF still did not have a program to account for personnel that would be in compliance with the Federal Department of Labor and State of Hawaii's labor laws.

But the PAF Board had discussed the need for a HR Division rather than the accountability of volunteers and project independent contractors by the external accountant.

PAF's vision at that time revolved around the number of PAF staff, limited by PAF's indirect cost rate, and the number of independent contract employees within the grant request.

PAF's Board tilted towards, first, resolving the indirect cost rate which would then, second, help to determine in large measure PAF's need for a HR division.

One of the strengths of a community nonprofit organization is its ability to limit its exposure to the many Federal and State regulations surrounding staff employees; the rules governing a nonprofit are designed to limit its overhead costs by restricting its indirect cost rate, thus limiting its exempt employees, and instead lean heavily on independent contractors who are identified and funded in the grant proposal.

Volunteers are passionate about the ideals of a project, want to contribute their skills, are community-focused; and while they are non-paid volunteers, the community nonprofit organization must have a paid dedicated and professional staff that can organize, coach and cheer on the work of dedicated, passionate volunteers.

Without such a staff, the efficiency and effectiveness of volunteers may be less than fulfilling.

And that is a burden the indirect cost rate does not yet recognize.

Operations. PAF's first-ever grant request submitted to the Queen Emma Foundation, written in coordination with the Director, Grants, Queen Emma Foundation, was limited to the project itself; that is, limited funding for the two grant investigators, one of whom would write the report, and restricted travel funding to selected minority healthcare centers principally in two states, Oregon and Washington.

The conduct of the project was focused on funding the research, analyses and report writing only; the final number and its consequent printing costs of the report were factored in to the grant funding request.

There were no costs programmed for an indirect cost rate that could be used for a PAF admin staff, accountant, office, office supplies, copy/scan/fax machine, computer equipment and parking; nor were costs allocated to cell phone usage, rental car, hotel accommodations, meals taxi fares, and baggage fees. Fortunately, personal credit cards absorbed many, if not all, of such expenses.

The operations approach of the grant request accommodated the funder's way of doing business – streamlined, focused and efficient.

This is normally the approach of most large 501(c)(3) nonprofit organizations that, in addition to approving its own community-focused projects, also provide grants to smaller community nonprofit organizations.

They are designed to use a percentage of their income,

usually generated through a large endowment or ownership of valuable land or commercial properties, which create substantial revenue for community-based projects that are consistent with their purposes and mission.

The non-funding of normal operational costs by the Queen Emma Foundation, while perhaps viewed as a conservative posture, is the approach that all nonprofits must understand is the way of business for community nonprofit organizations.

Community nonprofit organizations are not for-profits; should they adopt the techniques of for-profit businesses or large corporations, they must selectively do so.

Corporate nonprofit 501(c)(3) divisions have a wealth of techniques to raise funds and effective marketing practices to recruit skilled, dedicated, passionate volunteers who are strong advocates, and communicate that advocacy, in open forum.

Community nonprofit organizations, however, are structured for a minimal professional staff but with a data base of passionate donors, an even larger base of skilled doers, and a vast data base of volunteers who just want to contribute to their community, society and country in a way that is honorable and appreciated.

Conclusions. There are three take-away conclusions.

First, most community nonprofit organizations and public charities must think big but act humbly.

Community nonprofit organizations and public charities, as 501(c)(3) organizations like PAF, exist to selflessly serve others.

Understanding this principle leads directly to a strategic approach that minimizes infrastructure, maximizes the effectiveness and efficiency of the project itself, and points to the key factors that will strengthen a grant proposal.

The frustration that comes with a minimum indirect cost rate should never surface, as it (minimum indirect cost rate) is inherent in the term community nonprofit; when one mixes nonprofit indirect cost rate with for-profit's profit fee and G&A percentage, then confusion emerges, grows and becomes difficult to contain.

Second, effective and efficient management of community nonprofit 510(c)(3) organizations is, without question, the live-or-die-by reputation of community nonprofit organizations. Proper accounting, annual reviews and audits, financial systems, professional staff, reputable volunteers, involvement by the Board, legal advice, and complete buy-in by the nonprofit officers, oftentimes without cost or minimal cost to the nonprofit, are absolute requirements of any successful community nonprofit organization.

Third, the ethics and competence of the people executing the project are vital; their reputation, diligence and integrity are values a leader looks for in selecting doers, and this is true of the management of nonprofit projects or of the for-profit business of wealth creation. Building positive relationships is critical.

3. Loko I'a Kahinapohaku, Moloka'i

Native Hawaiian fishponds (*loko i'a*) dominated Hawaii's landscape prior to and a hundred years or so after Captain James Cook's arrival in Hawaii. Ancient chants and myths trace the *loko i'a* to the 14th century, probably in Egypt and other countries that bordered an ocean.

The *loko i'a's* of Hawaii were an engineering marvel, reflecting the Native Hawaiians' scholarship not only in science, technology, engineering and math but also in production management, biosecurity and environmental knowledge.

They were the early examples of what today is termed fish farming with various techniques and modern equipment designed for the lakes or open oceans.

Nearly five hundred (500) *loko i'a's* abounded in ancient Hawaii on the six islands of Maui, Oahu, Moloka'i, Kaua'i, Hawaii, and Lana'i with Moloka'i having the highest number of *loko i'a's* of which there were five types: loko wai, loko i'a kalo, loko pu'uone, loko kuapa and loko ume iki.

The *Kahinapohaku loko i'a* on the island of Molokai was a *loko kuapa* (seawall construction) of historic and cultural prominence, and in 1994 the community of Molokai worked diligently in developing a blueprint for the restoration of the more than 60 fishponds on Molokai with preferences given to five historic treasures, depending on the availability of Federal funding:

Oneali'i
Ualapu'e
Keawanu'i
Kahinapohaku
Honouliwai

While EPA provided the funding for the restoration and production revitalization of two *loko i'a's*, Honouliwai and Kahainapohaku, the PAF was selected to manage the Kahinapohaku *loko i'a* restoration and production revitalization.

Thus, in 1996 the PAF worked closely with the United

States Environment Protection Agency (EPA) which provided the funding, the community on Moloka'i that developed the blueprint, passionate Moloka'i Native Hawaiian leaders and a group of dedicated Moloka'i Native Hawaiian men and women without whom the project could never had withstood the quality inspection by a group of White House Fellows in 1998.

In the summer of 1998, the twelve (12) current White House Fellows visited Hawaii to specifically witness the restoration of Kahinapohaku loko i'a on the island of Molokai; and at the foot of the *loko i'a*, Kahinapohaku, one of the White House Fellows asked the relevant question:

> If this is a restored fishpond, where are the fishes?

Two of the Native Hawaiian leaders who escorted the White House Fellows looked at each other forlornly, and before either of them could utter a response, a school of fish swam in an organized formation a few meters from the standing group of White House Fellows, one of whom excitedly exclaimed:

> There they are!

Whether it was luck or the spirituality of Kahinapohaku or a blessing of the Native Hawaiian Gods or a miracle, it did happen.

Governance. The PAF was not fully prepared to move from its focus on healthcare to a community-designed blueprint of economic vitality based on the restoration of a *loko i'a*.

There were no *loko i'a* expertise nor skills nor competence nor science nor engineering knowledge among the two officers, the Native Hawaiian advisor or the four Board members.

While each was familiar with the importance of *loko i'a's* in food production, no one was familiar with the process or procedures in addressing the renovation of a *loko kuapa* which required the construction of a wall that could withstand the tidal action of the Pacific ocean.

There was a new Chair of the PAF Board, Kenneth F. Brown who brought wisdom, impeccable genealogy, passion and a revered reputation for excellence in all he undertook.

In accepting the responsibility and accountability of restoring and revitalizing Kahinapohaku, PAF also accepted the fiduciary requirements of EPA and Federal guidelines for accounting of the grant and project-end auditing, as well as the management duties of a Project Manager acceptable to the Native Hawaiian leaders and community on Molokai, for after all, they were the initiators of and provided compelling data for the project.

PAF was not involved in the 1994 community discussions that led to the blueprint nor the initial preparation and submission of the grant request to EPA.

Thus, PAF was asked to accept the grant because it had successfully executed two healthcare projects, and, more importantly, had been accepted by Native Hawaiian leaders on Molokai as an organization with whom they could work.

This last detail was the fulcrum point of the decision making process, but taken together, all factors were relevant in reaching a decision.

Thus, in 1996-1997, PAF undertook the responsibility to assist in the renovation of Kahinapohaku *loko i'a*.

The PAF officers and Board accepted the challenge, for how could it grow and develop to be true to its purposes if it were not for community-derived projects such as Kahinapohaku.

Financial Strategy. PAF accepted the budget submitted in the grant proposal and the financial reporting conditions; however, PAF was not provided an administrative fee, or its indirect cost rate, to purchase a software program for accounting and a payroll system, let alone pay for an accountant to track the costs, submit the required reports and prepare the financial statements for an external audit, all conditions required by EPA and fiduciary accountability.

The grant budget did allocate a wage rate for a Project Manager, limited travel and minimum funding to cover other operational expenses; but EPA did require dedicated oversight by PAF but not the funding to execute the required oversight.

Thus, for its third project, unlike the initial or the second project, PAF entered the execution phase of the grant project by having the operational details of a budget presented to it.

Accounting and External Audit. Integrating GAAP and Federal financial requirements with a culturally designed project staffed with independent-minded community activists, all of whom were honest, hard-working, dedicated and passionate regarding their project on the island of Molokai, was a responsible task.

While there were minor accounting details that may not have been in consonance with the grant accountability, they were not only inconsequential to regulatory requirements but overwhelmed by the goodness of the project and its outcome.

The President of PAF, along with the Project Manager, kept accurate accounting of each line of the grant, submitted the required reports, and kept an effective communication alive with the Native Hawaiian Molokai leaders, but especially the Native Hawaiian workforce who restored, hand carrying each and every rock, the loko i'a called Kahinapohaku.

Human Resources. PAF was not involved in the discussions nor design of the Molokai community blueprint for the restoration and revitalization of selected loko ia's nor in the initial development, writing and submission to EPA of the Kahinapohaku loko i'a grant request.

Hence, PAF could not impact the grant for building PAF's human resources infrastructure necessary to execute the project.

Operations. Assuming that the purpose and vision of the community project have been confirmed, then a vital aspect of operations is to start with the plans to execute the details of the project, then work backwards to generating a project budget.

PAF was fortunate in that the Moloka'i Native Hawaiian cultural leaders were closely affiliated with the Moloka'i Native Hawaiian workforce; and together they formed a bond to see the restoration and revitalization of Kahinapokahu loko i'a to its completion.

There already was a natural Native Hawaiian leader with whom PAF worked to ensure the daily targets were translated into specific activities of the project; for example, Kahinapohaku is a loko kuapa which required teaching the engineering skills of building the wall, and that instruction, which took nearly 2-3 weeks, was held on dry land for the entire Native Hawaiian workforce.

Another example was the selection of an experienced Native Hawaiian instructor by the Moloka'i Native Hawaiian leaders.

Safety of our worker force and working conditions were absolutely vital to the success of the project.

PAF selected an exceptional leader as the Project Manager to ensure compliance with the grant's conditions; the PM fulfilled the role of required of a superb communicator who facilitated the grantor's (EPA) compliance with the Moloka'i Native Hawaiian leaders and the Moloka'i Native Hawaiian workforce.

Finding and persuading such an outstanding PM was not an easy task; but fortunately the connectivity of relationships made the task doable.

Restoring a *loko i'a* requires various permits, a lengthy 6-step process for Federal agencies, a 6-step process for Hawaii State, a 3-step process for County, and an additional 7-step process for a State-owned *loko ia*; however, this confusing permitting process has since been made more streamlined, less intimidating, more timely and less bureaucratic; PAF, however, was not involved in designing a more effective and less cumbersome permitting procedure.

Conclusions. There are four factors that stand out in this project.

First, the PAF, though initially unprepared, overcame obstacles through perseverance and commitment to lead and manage this project. Safety was paramount.

Second, PAF was fortunate to have respected community leaders on Moloka'i who understood their culture and community needs which made it easier for PAF to accept accountability for this project.

Third, though PAF was unable to influence the grant budget to accommodate PAF's indirect cost rate, PAF was able, with great assistance from many others, to fulfill the Federal compliance demanded of nonprofit organizations.

Fourth, though PAF had not established any project past performance relationship with the Molokai Native Hawaiian cultural leaders nor with those who prepared and submitted the grant request, PAF had great confidence and trust in those who had the vision to restore its community cultural pride, the *loko ia*.

4. National Pacific American Leadership Institute (NAPALI)

The concept for cultural leadership was directly implied in the purposes of the Pacific American Foundation, one
of which is leadership.

Therefore, in 1997 with the assistance of an allied consultant, the President, PAF, met with Peter Drucker, founder of Claremont Graduate School of Management which became Claremont Graduate University in 1971. And within a two-hour discussion at Claremont on leadership and management ("management is doing things right; leadership is doing the right things"- Peter F. Drucker, The Essential Drucker), an agreement was reached in which Claremont Graduate School of Management would sponsor the first class of Fellows of the newly formed Pacific American Emerging Leaders Program (PAEL) in the early fall of 1997.

Thus was born the PAF's Pacific American Emerging Leaders Program, and the first class of nine (9) Fellows who spent six days at Claremont Graduate School of Management undergoing a course designed as the first cultural leadership program in our country, for as Peter Drucker said to the PAF President:

> With all the brilliant PhD's at Claremont Graduate School of Management, not one advanced the idea of cultural leadership as you have done.

The first PAF cultural leadership class was composed of 13 Fellows - 9 Native Hawaiians of whom one was a female, 2 American Samoans, and two Chamorros.

Senior leadership included Al Pauole, Executive Director, PAF; Clint Helenihi, Class Monitor; Andrea McAleenan, Claremont Graduate School of Management; and a delegation from American Samoa.

Between 1997-2005, PAF conducted approximately twice-yearly cultural leadership courses at Kapi'olani Community College (KCC), Honolulu, Hawaii.

Between 2005-2017 once-yearly courses, approximately, was taught at Kapi'olani Community College, but instead of being termed the Pacific American Emerging Leaders Program, the name of the course changed to National Pacific American Leadership Institute, or NAPALI.

Governance. PAF formed the Pacific American Emerging Leaders Program because conditions were right, and the PAF officers and Board were in agreement to initiate a cultural leadership course.

The two PAF officers had begun discussions with Native Hawaiian community leaders to start a cultural leadership course for emerging Pacific American leaders between the ages of 28-35 from across the country, including American Samoa and Guam; the class size was set between 12-15 Fellows, and the course was designed to expose the Fellows to the academic language of leadership by Professors from the Department of Arts and Sciences, University of Hawaii-Manoa; the cultural traditions of Native Hawaiians, American Samoans, Tongans, Chamorros by cultural practitioners, to include visits to cultural sites; current active leaders of the State Legislature, Congressional Delegation, Kamehameha Schools, Office of Hawaiian Affairs, and First Hawaiian Bank; panels of experienced leaders and managers of nonprofit organizations, Federal agencies and commercial businesses; and full participation by the Fellows in naming their class as well as defining their personal path over the next several years.

The course has been modified on occasion, as Harvard Graduate students were permitted to join the cultural leadership program; involvement by various cultural entertainers; participation by the Polynesian Voyaging Society, and changes in location.

The PAF President had also begun discussions in 2001 with the executive leadership of Pacific American Emerging Leaders Program to consider establishing a separate 501(c)(3), thus allowing the leadership program to seek its own funds, start its own governing structure, launch its own identity, and align itself with the Pacific American Foundation.

Hence, in 2004 the Pacific American Emerging Leaders Program became NAPALI, submitted its 501(c)(3) application which was approved by the IRS, and initiated its own fund raising strategies.

Today NAPALI enjoys an immensely successful cultural leadership program that has attracted attention by other national leadership programs, as LEAP, and delights in the reputation earned by the graduating approximately 260 Fellows who have gone on to not only successful careers in education, politics, community organizations, businesses, corporations and research centers but also have received several distinguished acknowledgements for their contributions.

Financial Strategy. PAF had limited funding in its banking account, and thus was unable to set aside the full cost to pay for the first cultural leadership course.

PAF had not submitted a grant request to any Federal agency or a private nonprofit organization as it had no time once Peter Drucker agreed to support the PAF's first ever cultural leadership course at Claremont Graduate School of Management, Claremont, CA.

Because of the personal commitment by Peter Drucker, the Executive Director of Claremont Graduate School of Management absorbed the costs of the set up and for all breakfasts, lunches, dinners and classroom space for the entire 6 days.

The Executive Director also arranged with the nearby hotel for preferential room costs as well as with buses for local travel; this cost avoidance allowed PAF to absorb the remainder of the costs for airfare travel, lodging and rental cars; Clint Helehini, Class Monitor, provided at no cost the Native Hawaiian musical groups that created a unique cultural environment at Claremont.

Accounting and External Audit. PAF had not yet established an accounting or audit system; the PAF President accepted this risk as the personal support by

Peter Drucker and the full involvement of Claremont Graduate School of Management made the launch of the Pacific American Emerging Leaders Program, not only privileged and fortunate, but also very timely.

Human Resources. PAF still did not have a human resources Director nor a personnel system to accommodate payroll, employee validation, vacation nor a program of benefits. But the emerging leaders program, though discussed at various times with the PAF Board, took on the fortuitous nature of just materializing because of a 2-hour meeting; and the decision to launch the Pacific America Emerging Leaders Program was, although risky, providential.

Operations. The PAF officers and Board had several discussions regarding the start of a cultural leadership course, and steps had been taken to identify the attendees, support team and the course itself. But there was no operational plan from which to adjust; PAF was given the opportunity when a door opened, and the PAF officers took it and walked through the door.

Conclusions. There are five lessons learned from this project:

1. Never turn down a meeting because you never know what will come of the meeting. Establishing and sustaining relationships developed through trust and confidence are absolutely critical.

2. Risk decision making occurs when you least expect it; while you must have a risk management plan, there are times when risks should not be the decisive factor nor unduly influence the leader's decision.

3. Funding a project is an art and a skill; when there is no approved budget, it is far better to understand the major cost factors than lose the tipping point because there is no budget, let alone an approved budget.

4. If there is unanimity for the vision and purpose of a project, proceed with vigor.

5. PAF was better prepared to undertake this project as it had a draft plan of the types of candidates, the course itself, and the support team. Though PAF was not fully prepared to launch the cultural leadership course when it did, it had the leadership experience in education and Pacific American cultures to serve as core instructors and knew and understood the Native values around which the curriculum was based.

Chapter 3. The For-Profit Years, 2004 – 2017, Hui O Hana Pono

Native Hawaiian Organization (NHO)

In 2001 discussions were held between the Hawaii Congressional Delegation and the SBA office in Honolulu regarding the establishment of a Native Hawaiian business organization that would have similar, if not the same, government contracting authorities as the Native American Tribes (Tribes) and the Alaskan Native Corporations (ANC).

After several planning strategies and changes in directions, the Native Hawaiian Organization (NHO) was born in 2003 with similar government contracting authorities as the Native American Tribes and Alaskan Native Corporations; parity with the Tribes and ANCs was a bridge too far politically as the Native Hawaiians did not have a treaty, unlike the Tribes and ANCs, signed between the Kingdom and the United States Congress.

Thus, the NHO was structured as a nonprofit organization with 8(a) small disadvantaged for-profit businesses, not quite the same as the Native American Tribes or the Alaska Native Corporation.

The NHO is supervised by the U.S. Small Business Administration, and consequently the NHO is vigilantly regulated by the Federal Acquisition Regulation (FAR) and SBA's statutes and rules.

In 2005 the second NHO, Hui O Hana Pono, was approved by the U.S. Small Business Administration after the Hui had submitted its application in November 2004.

The business case analyses of the four for-profit

contracts of the Hui are among the more than fifty contracts won by the Hui over a period of twelve (12) years, 2005-2017.

As mentioned earlier, the same three Native Hawaiians, Irwin K. Cockett, Alvin H. Pauole, and David EK Cooper, were the principal decision makers for the Hui as they are the Hui's Board of Directors, just as they served on the Board of the Pacific American Foundation from 1993-2004.

There was a fourth person, Michael Beasley, brilliant and experienced, who provided a safety net of wisdom, substantial operational guidance and sensible business advice from 1993-2017.

1. Navy Security Contracts.

The Pearl Harbor Security contract was one of three security contracts, which were bundled into one contract, awarded in 2005 to the Hui's Joint Venture with the Hana Group as the Managing Partner and Day & Zimmerman as the minority partner.

The three security contracts were the Naval Air Station at Maine with contract execution March 2005; the Groton Naval Base, CT with contract execution May 2005, and the Pearl Harbor Naval Base, HI with contract execution September 2005.

Each contract was independent of each other, geographically dispersed and required not only recruiting, hiring, training, equipping, weapons, vehicles, scheduling of shifts, personnel accountability but also contract management, safety and quality control plans, payroll system, financial management, operational policies and procedures, and experienced Project Managers, Site Supervisors and Shift Supervisors.

All three contracts taxed the embryonic capabilities, assets and resources of the Hana Group who had just been established and approved by SBA in February 2005 as an NHO.

Governance. The Hana Group, Inc., had just been approved by SBA as an 8(a) company in February 2005 and simultaneously approved the NHO, a nonprofit registered in the State of Hawaii, under the name of Hui O Hana Pono.

The Hana Group, Inc., had one officer, the President.

The NHO nonprofit, Hui O Hana Pono, was comprised of three Board members.

But there was a brilliant ally, an attorney with a common touch through his communication skills, Michael Beasley, who provided concrete business guidance and sound legal advice to the Hui Board.

But fortunately, the Hana Group and Day & Zimmerman applied for SBA's Mentor Protégé Program, and with the approval of SBA, formed a Joint Venture to manage the newly awarded contract.

A Joint Venture Management group, consisting of two members from Hana Group and one member from Day & Zimmerman, was established and met weekly to assess our compliance to the three contract sites. It was brilliantly led by Brad Cooper.

Financial Strategy. Neither The Hana Group, Inc., nor Hui O Hana Pono, had yet formed a financial strategy, accounting management system, internal or external audit processes, cash flow analysis procedure, or any financial administrative controls. At the time of the award, the Hana Group was in the process of establishing a bank account.

An investment was made for the start-up capital requirements; and with this investment, a bank account was established.

Once the contract was signed, Hana Group realized that a G&A fee amounted to an annual dollar amount, and the Board decided to rent an office space, allocate travel expenses, purchase the necessary office equipment and computer systems as well as the appropriation of sufficient funds for the three PMs and their support teams.

Accounting and External Audit. At the time of the award, neither The Hana Group, Inc., nor Hui O Hana Pono had yet established an accounting or external audit system.

However, once the investment was final, progress was made towards hiring a CFO, financial manager and an accountant; and a financial management system was installed.

The first order of business was to establish a payroll system followed by accounting procedures that were in accordance with GAAP, payment of taxes and internal and external audits.

Human Resources. Prior to the time of the approval of the NHO by SBA, discussions had already begun among the Hui Board to recruit a Director, Human Resources; with the award of the very first Hana Group contract, the call to action had become more spirited.

The President, Hana Group, Inc., hired a full time Director, Human Resources once the investment was finalized and the G&A calculations were confirmed. The Hui Board acknowledged that an Assistant Director, Human Resources, would be necessary for the mainland contracts, and moved to hire an Assistant within weeks after the contract award.

Operations. Because these three contracts, bundled as one contract, were awarded to the Hana Group, Inc, the 8(a) SD business of the NHO, Hui O Hana Pono, within three months of SBA's approval of Hana Group and the NHO, there was no time set aside to develop an operational plan to execute these three dispersed contracts.

The Hana Group started a contract geographically dispersed among three states, accepted the challenge, and took positive steps to institute positive outcomes.

It took all three Board members, working 24/7, to manage this enormously diverse opportunity; fortunately, SBA had approved the Hana/Day & Zimmerman Mentor Protégé application, and together we formed a Joint Venture with the establishment of a Management Group to handle the day to day contract requirements at three different sites.

We took steps to hire trustworthy, experienced Project Managers in each of the three locations; and then depended on them to hire a team of trustworthy, experienced Site Supervisors and Shift Supervisors to ensure our compliance with contract requirements and standards of performance.

The geographic dispersion caused more distresses than we had the skilled management or experienced operators to anticipate or to resolve immediately.

Our inattention and lack of experience in leading and managing geographically dispersed sites, in addition to our ignoring of a basic rule...trust but check...led to very challenging times.

The Hui Board Directors, Irv Cockett, Al Pauole and Dave Cooper, with the superb assistance of Mike Beasley, understood the nature of the challenge, worked with other distinguished leaders and managers, and found the right solutions without disciplining anyone, for as leaders, we believed we were as much at fault as those who were accountable.

Conclusions. There are many conclusions that can be drawn from this experience, but the four that stand out in the analysis are these:

1. Opportunities must be judged on their tendency to be financially negative but simultaneously contribute positively to the organization's vision.

2. Presented with a contract which had all the markings of immense difficulties, look first to prioritizing the problems; second, apply your team's skills to overcome the challenges but be aware that the solution may require others with more experience and skill; and third, never reduce your aggressiveness on Safety and the health of your work force.

3. Smile when awarded a bundled contract for which your company is without any current financial, administrative or operational capabilities.

4. Install a system of checks and balances, ask questions, and should results appear unsettling or if your instinct suggests a problem, investigate immediately using external, qualified examiners.

2. **Server Consolidation**

Within several months of the Navy Security contract award, Hana Group, in a Joint Venture with Day & Zimmerman, teamed with IBM to win the CNIC Server Consolidation contract.

The technology requirements were not burdensome as IBM provided the skilled technicians while the Hana Group, as the Managing Partner of the Joint Venture, developed the operational plan that included objectives, timelines, metrics to measure progress and reports management.

The IBM's representative had been fully involved with the details as well as the project's presentation to CNIC, and thus was fully on board with the operational measures of success.

The award was a sole source contract made by the Contracting Officer who possessed the authority to make such award, such authority being a strength of the NHO.

Governance. The Hana Group, Inc., and the Hui Board, had the same Board Directors, thus making it easier for decision making.

The President, Hana Group, Inc., had brought on board two staff members with offices in Honolulu as well as an Assistant Director, Human Resources and a staff member in the office in Philadelphia, and office provided by our legal counsel, in addition to the financial and accounting team.

The Joint Venture established a Management Group consisting of two Hana personnel and one from our minority partner, Day & Zimmerman, to manage the project. Our IBM representative fully participated in the sessions of the Management Group, but without a vote.

Financial Strategy. The CNIC Server Consolidation contract was established as a Cost Plus contract which required a different invoicing and accounting by Hana's financial team; the Management Group, along with Hana, Day & Zimmerman and IBM's accounting departments, accomplished the Cost Plus contract's requirements with flying colors.

During this period Hana Group undertook the task of securing a line of credit with Citizens Bank, Philadelphia; it was a complex undertaking, but the Hui Board realized that without a line of credit, the first 60-90 days of executing a contract will continue to be difficult.

Having two Federal contracts, one for armed security at three dispersed locations and one for Information Technology, allowed Hana, and the Hui, to plan for sustained infrastructure improvements.

For example, Hana brought on a pricing person to begin a process to effectively capture future solicitations, and contracted with an independent firm to assist us in establishing a 401K Program.

We were informed by DCAA (Defense Contract Audit Agency (DCAA) that they would conduct an audit of our G&A percentage and transactions, a normal procedure; we welcomed their external audit.

Accounting and External Audit. With this second Federal contract, Hana Group and the Hui Board began to initiate a formal financial system, including payroll that tracks vacation time and paid time off; a 401K program without matching; unfunded requirements; and a monthly financial statement that tracked every expense.

The Hana and Hui Boards instituted a vendor contract for an external audit of our accounting system, filing of our Federal and State Tax Returns, and audit of our 401K program.

Human Resources. Both Hana and Hui Boards realized that our Human Resources section would be stretched to negotiate managed-healthcare benefits for our contract employees, some of whom were Service Contract Act (SCA) employees and some of whom were Collective Bargaining Agreement (CBA) employees, as well as Hana Group, Inc., staff members.

We also recognized that Human Resources would need to be reinforced to handle the complex recruiting so vital to the type of contracts we plan to pursue...physical security with levels of security classification; specialty skills in Information Technology; highly specialized skills in the engineering and range operations domain; functional experts in base facilities operations; and administrative professionals in various staff augmentation fields.

We believed we would be competitive in the Federal contracting arena.

Operations. While the Hana President, the Hana and Hui Boards worked tirelessly to understand the technology aspects of the contract, it was the Management Group appointed by the Joint Venture that managed the day to day operations of the contract.

The Management Group accommodated the phased plan's requirements and accomplished the objectives within the time allocated for the contract.

At the end of the project, the CNIC commended the team for its outstanding performance.

Conclusions. We can take away five conclusions from this contract:

1. Have a vision, and communicate the vision of where you want your business to be at each 5 year-point...5, 10, 15, 20, 25; be as definitive as you can but recognize that changes happen.

2. Welcome contracts for which you are unprepared but from which you are eager to learn.

3. Build a business infrastructure as soon as you can, developing each simultaneously, starting with finance and accounting followed by HR followed by operations.

4. Be prepared to conduct reviews and analyses, ask questions, trust but institute wise checks.

5. Understand the value of a management committee and the importance of technology contracts in building your skills base.

3. Conventional Prompt Global Strike

The opportunity to expand the Hui's technical capabilities arrived with Dr. Barry Hannah, Deputy Director, Strategic Systems Program (SSP), U.S. Navy, who believed that a Native Hawaiian 8(a) company had to be involved in SSP's project to develop a strategic weapon system, primarily because the flight testing would involve the Pacific Missile Range Facility on Kaua'i, Hawaii.

The Hui's Chair and a Director began a discussion with Dr. Hannah in 2012, and by 2013 a 2-year contract was awarded to the Hana Group for staff augmentation support to SSP to develop key documents and participate as a member in several significant planning groups who would principally meet at Sandia Labs, Alburqurque, NM.

Governance. At this point in the Hui's development, SBA had already approved the second 8(a) company, Hana Business and Management Consulting (HBC), whose President also held the Vice Chair position on the Hui Board.

Thus, the Hui had two 8(a) companies, Hana Group, Inc., and HBC, with each President also serving on the Company Board that had the same complement as Hui Board Directors, three members.

The unofficial fourth member was Michael Beasley.

There were no other officers in each company, as SBA had acknowledged that in accordance with Hawaii laws, the President could also simultaneously hold the positions of Secretary and Treasurer.

By 2012 the Hui had an established an exempt team of a 4-member finance and accounting division; a 2-member Human Resources division; a Facility Security Officer (FSO); a 2-member Capture Center; a 3-member operations division; and a dedicated external law firm negotiated through an annual retainer fee.

Financial Strategy. An investment was made towards the start-up financial requirements of HBC.

The Hui had been operational for seven years; underwent three Defense Contract Audit Agency (DCAA) audits regarding our G&A percentage, as well as a Defense Contract Management Center (DCMC) audit on our Server Consolidation contract because it was issued as a Cost Plus contract; an annual external audit of its accounting and finance procedures; monthly financial statements which included a Profit and Loss Statement; and cash contributions to support Native Hawaiian programs totaling approximately $500,000.

The establishment with Citizens Bank of a $5,000,000 Line of Credit was more than sufficient to handle the first 90-days of this contract.

Accounting and Audit. The 4-member accounting and finance team had moved to an adjacent office provided by our legal counsel who was headquartered in Philadelphia, PA, and they were competent and operational from day one.

Human Resources. The Assistant Director, Human Resources, had a desk among the 4-member accounting and finance team; and instantly he was an essential participant in recruiting the IT skills needed for the contract.

The Project Manager, Troy Cooper, was brilliant in leading and managing the complex contract, made even more difficult because the IBM experts were in three different States

Operations. The Project Manager divided the execution of the contract into three phases with specific tasks, objectives and reports; especially complicated was the daily tracking of the scope of work laid out by the actions that were supportive of the contract's factors and sub-factors.

The Project Manager introduced the concept of Performance Work Statement (PWS) that defined every action within a timeline against a time sheet for every employee assigned to the contract. It became the tracking mechanism used by the Joint Venture

Management Group to ensure the contract would be successfully completed, on time and within the funding provided.

Conclusions. We can derive three conclusions applicable to this contract:

1. Teaming Agreements with minority partners or subcontractors must be specific regarding scope of work that is easily transferrable to percentages of work from which a dollar value can be attached.

2. Even with substantial staff capabilities, managing change can be complex.

3. Knowledge regarding the specifics of the scope of work is critical, but leadership is vital.

4. <u>Army Tree Trimming</u>

This was a new work function for the Hui who eleven years ago in response to a question by a senior NAVFAC acquisition specialist, Lynn Wong:

> What do you all do?

Al Pauole replied:

> We do everything from cutting grass to shooting missiles.

This contract completed Al Pauole's answer, and in retrospect hopefully complements the laughter by all that bounced off the walls of the room that morning in Honolulu.

Army Tree Trimming was a difficult bidding activity as we had no past experience writing the technical nor how to price the various types of trees in the scope of work; the RFP was much too general in nature that writing to the strengths of the Hui's companies was difficult, let alone attempting a pricing proposal based on an Indefinite Delivery and Indefinite Quantities (IDIQ) contract requirements rather than established contract objectives.

We elected to bring in a subcontractor, South Pacific, who had several years of tree trimming experience, especially in pricing IDIQ contracts, which was the focus of this solicitation.

Governance. After nearly ten (10) years of government contract awards and performances in various industries...security, range operations, staff augmentation, information technology, base operations, facilities management, warehouse operations, missile technology, business information systems, security escort services, server consolidation...and three SBA Mentor Protégé Programs, several subcontracts and a focus on funding programs in support of principally Native Hawaiians in Hawaii, the Hui had established the required staff support systems and designed a progressive vision of where the Hui would like to be in 5-year segments.

Despite the Hui's ten (10) year experience, we did not specifically follow our process in forming partnerships; and it was a shortcoming that became a challenge within the first year of contract performance.

Financial Strategy. The Hui had developed the appropriate financial and banking systems to support this contract, though we had little experience in understanding the financial impacts of an Indefinite Delivery and Indefinite Quantities (IDIQ) contract.

Our Honolulu team recommended we align ourselves

to South Pacific, a small business in Honolulu with experience in tree trimming operations. We did.

Accounting and Audit. The Hui had a solid, competent accounting team who had undergone ten (10) external audits by a certified firm, as well as having undergone three (3) DCCA and one (1) DCMC audits. The results were impressive.

Human Resources. We had little experience in identifying or recruiting the skill sets of tree trimmers; it was a new experience for our HR Division, but armed with previous recruiting experiences over the past ten (10) years, our HR team knew how to think about resolving the challenge which was made easier by teaming with South Pacific.

Operations. We did not prepare a Teaming Agreement with a specific Exhibit A that defined the scope of work, the percentage of work, the equipment to be provided, the support expected or all the details required of any subcontractor.

The absence of a Teaming Agreement led to a communication shortcoming – our failure to prepare and execute a subcontract.

Additionally, we experienced safety issues and maintenance shortcomings in executing this contract.

We pursued this contract to support our vision in Hawaii; in retrospect, we should have been better prepared to diligently execute our contract's compliance, safety and maintenance plans.

Perhaps this contract brought home the reality of safety and maintenance, both in the planning for and the daily execution of safety and maintenance; nothing brings fear to a leader except when he sees an unsafe act, or the cost of time when an equipment has not been maintained properly and impacts productivity.

Conclusions. There are several conclusions that can be drawn from this contract.

1. The established capture process must be expressly followed by all.

2. The lack of a definitive Teaming Agreement led to the absence of a subcontract which resulted in communication challenges.

3. The execution of the contract depended on the prime and subcontractor working as a team.

4. The absence of a specific plan of operations led to a breakdown in contract compliance.

5. Any less than a dedicated compliance to follow the Safety and Quality Control Plans leads to inevitable incidents.

Chapter 4. Five Steps To Success

The eight projects selected for analysis represent a variety of functional purposes and different degrees of success. The primary factor in their selection rests in the comparative analysis among the eight.

Each, however, tells a story that allows its own analysis.

But for the reader, the strength of the conclusions is two-fold:

1. The analysis of each project as a standalone project.

2. A comparative analysis of all eight projects.

Using the same comparative factors for every one of the eight (8) projects, the findings point to the five steps to success, whether leading and managing a community nonprofit organization or a for-profit business.

Values

Nothing shines brighter or shatters more quickly than ethics; there is good wealth to be earned and bad wealth to be avoided.

When your competitor commends your actions that reflect doing what is right when no one is watching, he is validating what your colleagues, staff, employees and work force already know.

There is no substitute for standards, not 100% but beyond 100%; measure what your team accomplishes by the standards, not of the grant or the contract requirements, but what and how you encouraged the team to reach beyond their grasp.

Values ought not to be legislated, but worn like a cloak around your shoulders; who you are is a reflection of your beliefs, principles and ideals.

Never leave a genuine spirit of thankfulness with a great deal of respect for others in your bottom desk drawer or in your back pocket; let your smile shine brightly.

The spirit of teamwork is the common denominator of leaders of community nonprofit organizations and for-profit businesses.

Trust but Check

Develop mutual trust based on relationships but develop mutual trust based on astute business deeds.

Relationships that lead to mutual trust can, hopefully, grow into trust and confidence in the business world; and while they seem synonymous, mutual trust in the business world is based on a simple factor of confidence.

Hope, potential, probability, likelihood, possibility, promise, expectation and anticipation equate to pyrrhic victories.

As Executive Director of community nonprofit organizations or CEO of for-profit businesses, confidence is built with many mini steps until one can take a giant leap. It frankly works for any leader.

A community nonprofit organization or a for-profit business, intent on growing its assets, must first ensure it has embedded the protective measures that can secure its reputation and resources.

People trust people until they prove otherwise; and while you should initially extend such trust, install checks and balances that protect those whom you trust.

But realize that there are a very few who will leverage your basic trust into their personal bank accounts.

Change Is A Constant Factor

There are few things in leading community nonprofits or for-profit businesses that equate to the sun rising in the early morning or setting in the late evening; and one of those few things is change that happens nearly every day.

Changes are embedded in the very nature of leadership. How a leader thinks about changes impact not only the solutions but also the environment and attitude of those who are faced with handling changes.

Change shuts a window but opens a door; seeing both and communicating the options that change brings are critical to positive leadership.

Stability in leading community nonprofits and for-profit businesses involves change. While we hope for smooth sailing in all endeavors, leadership must treat successes and defeats equally for each brings its own set of challenges as each is a change in itself.

As Samuel Clemmons has mentioned in one of his wise sayings, even when one is sitting on the right track, one can be run over as the train is still coming.

Balance Ego With Humility

Success of a for-profit business generally leads to economic strength; success for a community nonprofit organization generally leads to community strength; these strengths generally lead to power; and power unchecked expressly leads to inexcusable actions.

No Executive Director nor CEO who share the same passion to serve others can ever fall victim to excessive ego, for if they do, then those whom they serve will be irreparably harmed.

There is no such thing as win or go home when one has the passion to serve, and that is the one factor that works for both the Executive Director and the CEO.

Developing and maintaining genuine relationships demand an honesty and professionalism that are reflected in your smile, handshake, standards, safety program, quality control policies, teamwork and commitment to compliance of all requirements in the agreement or contract. The right approach is when you put the customer's concerns ahead of yours; then trust and confidence grows geometrically.

Leadership - Steel Fist Wrapped In a Velvet Glove

Leadership is unequivocally the one, single factor that is explicitly shared between the Executive Directors of community nonprofit organizations and the CEOs of for-profit businesses.

The analyses of the eight (8) business cases leave no doubt that without leaders who are energetic, positive in outlook, genuinely care about people, competent, understand numbers, see beyond the horizon, and are effective in verbal and written communications, then the other four "what works" above are superfluous.

Leading a community nonprofit organization or a for-profit business demands clear outcomes and goals; a vision statement is absolutely necessary, but it must also be followed by specific objectives over a specific time schedule, be it months or by phasing over a period of time. By developing a strategic philanthropy, you impact people's lives; by developing a strategic goal, you return stock values to the shareholders.

But when you as a leader combine selfless service with economic engines, you impact the world.

The representation of a "steel fist wrapped in a velvet glove" is a powerful image in the American epic poem, John Brown's Body, written by Stephen Vincent Benet in 1928.

And it is a fitting picture of what works today, 89 years later.

Chapter 5. The Challenges Beyond

Those who seek self-determination should recognize that flag waving, protest movements, parades on main street or attempting to manage the media may be necessary, initially, to raise others' awareness of the issue or the concern of inequality.

But they do not eventually change public policy.

Only an elected, governing body politic is empowered with the accountability and responsibility, and the implementing agencies, to formulate and enforce public policy.

To encourage action by the elected body politic takes planning, resources, education, information and statistics that are credible; and passionate leadership linked to economic engines that have the similar, or identical, values of community nonprofit organizations.

Relying on community nonprofit organizations who argue passionately for the underserved or for those who lack access is only part of the solution; leaders who lead a community nonprofit organization are heroes simply because they lead with very little resources but with a great passion to serve.

However, by combining the values, competence, work ethic, communication skills of passionate leaders of community nonprofit organizations with the values, competence, work ethic, communication skills of passionate for-profit leaders, then the magic begins.

The magic begins to happen when there is real economic strength that derives its foundation from the values of community nonprofit service; one cannot survive without the linking to the other; but certainly for underserved populations and minority groups, having economic engines that contribute to creating healthy communities are vital to sustaining a passion to selfless service.

There is more "what works" alikeness between the community nonprofit and for-profit leaders than imagined 96 years ago when President Warren G. Harding signed into law the Hawaiian Homes Commission Act of 1921.

The quest for self-determination and sovereignty by either indigenous or minority groups begins with economics devoted to service, economics empowered by the passion of selfless service.

Endnotes, Chapter 1

1. The author was a Military Fellow at the Council of Foreign Relations, 1984–1985, and attended the CFR luncheon for the President, American Express.

2. The author was a participant in the study group during 1984–1985 that collaborated on the data that was published by Dankwart A. Rostow in the book, Turkey: America's Forgotten Ally, 1987.

3. The author was invited by Kahu Abraham Akaka to a meeting in January 1994 at the Coral Ballroom, Hilton Hawaiian Village, Honolulu, HI. The three questions Kahu Akaka asked Booze Allen Hamilton to address and the story of his Tutuwahine are as he described and remembered by the author.

4. The author has worked with all the cited Native Hawaiian cultural and business leaders, including Robert Oshiro, except with Mary Kawena Pukui, David Malo and Samuel Kamakau, the last two who were early recorders of Native Hawaiian issues in the 19th century.

5. The author wrote the essay, "The Quest for Sovereignty in the Pacific" which was published, among other essays prepared by the study group led by Kiichi Mochizuki, in the book, Taiwan Independence and Limitations to the Nation-State Concept. The author was invited to deliver his essay in Japan in October 1996 to an assembled audience of Japanese business executives.

6. The author used Wikipedia to cite quotations of the history of the Hawaiian Homes Commission Act of 1921, the Apology Resolution and the Akaka Bill.

7. The author is the founder of the Pacific American Foundation and served as its President from 1994 to 2004.

Endnotes, Chapter 2

1. The author is the founder of the Pacific American Foundation and served as its President from 1994 through 2004. The author was fully involved with all functions and aspects of the Foundation during these years.

2. The author met with the Queens Healthcare Systems Board in March 1994 and presented the initiative of a healthcare summit in Honolulu attended by healthcare, political and business leaders from Hawaii, American Samoa and Guam with a follow-on report to every member of the United States Congress; the recollections are as accurate as the author recalls, to include Bob Oshiro's pragmatic and practical question.

3. The author worked with the Queen Emma Foundation in preparing the grant request.

4. The author and Al Pauole were the principal investigators and visited at least two-three minority healthcare centers to gather data that were included in the report, "Minority Healthcare Centers – Best Practices and Techniques," written by the author.

5. The title of the report, "Pacific Americans and The National Healthcare Act: Where We Fit,"

was suggested by Robert Alm, Vice President, Community Affairs, Queens Healthcare Systems.

6. The author and Walter Ritte were the two Native Hawaiians escorting the White House Fellows to Kahinapohaku *loko i'a*; the question asked by a White House Fellow stunned both the author and Walter, but the arrival of the school of fish within seconds of the question was not imagined; neither was the exclamation of the White House Fellow.

7. The report, "Pacific Americans and The National Healthcare Act: Where We Fit," was jointly written by Ben Pangelinan, a Native Chamorro member of the Guam Legislature, Tommy Kaulukukui, Robbie Alm and the author who also was the principal designer and editor of the report. Robbie Alm suggested the title, led the printing and production of the report.

8. Andrea McAleenan, Executive Director, Claremont Graduate School of Management, arranged for the meeting between the author and Peter Drucker in his home; Andrea joined us, and we ended the discussion approximately two hours later with Drucker's clear commitment to support the PAF's first cultural leadership course at Claremont Graduate School of Management. Peter Drucker's comment is quoted by the author as the author recalls the comment.

9. Several donors helped to defray the other costs or the first cultural leadership course.

10. NAPALI is a separate 501(c)(3), led today by incredibly passionate and competent Native

Hawaiian cultural leaders as Heather and Frank Minton, Wanda and Larry Kamahele, Reidar and Sharon Smith, David and Marilyn Burge and others who have gone before, as Clint and Susan Helenihi, Irwin Cockett, Al Pauole and the author and his wife, Katherine. Apologies to many others, whose names I cannot recall, not mentioned here

Endnotes, Chapter 3.

1. The author founded Hana Engineering, Inc., in 1994 which later became an 8(a) SD company approved by the U.S. Small Business Administration in 2005; Hana Engineering then became The Hana Group, Inc., in 2006.

2. The author also founded the second Native Hawaiian Organization (NHO) with the formation of the nonprofit organization, Hui O Hana Pono, both of which was approved by the U.S. Small Business Administration in 2005; the State of Hawaii's Department of Commerce and Consumer Affairs approved Hui O Hana Pono as a state nonprofit organization in 2005.

3. Irwin Cockett, Al Pauole and the author were the NHO's Board members since its inception in 2005; all three were also the PAF's Board members from 1995 to 2004.

4. Michael Beasley assisted the author in executing the Pacific American Foundation's registration in the State of Virginia and has been the PAF's General Counsel and Secretary from its inception in 1993.

5. Michael Beasley has been a valuable leader, manager, staff member and Project Manager

for Hui O Hana Pono since 2005, and continues his immense contributions to the many activities of the NHO Hui O Hana Pono.

6. The author was joined by Al Pauole at the Navy Yard, Washington, DC in persuading Maggie Gervais to award a sole source contract for Navy security at the Naval Air Station, ME; Groton Naval Station, CT; and Pearl Harbor, HI. The Navy security contract was negotiated by the author, Day & Zimmerman and Maggie Gervais.

7. The author and Boodi Blanc, IBM, briefed CNCI representatives regarding our capabilities to execute CNIC's requirement to consolidate its severs; CNIC awarded the contract as a sole source to the Joint Venture created by The Hana Group and Day & Zimmerman; but the project was brilliantly executed by Troy Cooper as the PM and the Joint Venture Management Committee led by Bradley Cooper.

8. Dr. Barry Hannah, Deputy Director, Strategic Systems Program (SSP), U.S. Navy, and the author initiated discussions, which later included Al Pauole, to structure the NHO's involvement in SSP's new mission to develop a strategic missile system. After several one-on-one sessions with the senior leaders of SSP, the NHO was awarded a staff augmentation contract that is brilliantly led today by Michael Beasley, the PM.

9. Mike Rawlins, Michael Cooper, and Andrew Dash prepared the technical proposal; and with the help of Bruce Jacobsen, South Pacific, finalized the pricing proposal.

10. Admiral Ken Fisher, former President, Hana Industries; Brad Cooper, COO; Mike Rawlins, Director of Pacific Operations; and Michael Cooper, Project Manager, have managed this contract with success to date; and the financial, safety and maintenance outlook is positive.

Endnotes, Chapter 4.

1. The author, as an Assistant Professor of English, United States Military Academy, 1974-1977, taught Stephen Vincent Benet's American epic poem, <u>John Brown's Body</u>, as a course requirement of Plebe English; the image is one of the author's favorites.